"Being transparent is difficult for most people. We work at looking and speaking lik[...] this book, for its honesty in the reality of life. *Blooming in the Dark* is a must read as we face trials and difficulties along the way. Thanks, Bonnie, for sharing your journey."

—Carolyn Suty
U.S. Regional Director for Aglow International

"As I read the stories and prayers shared so beautifully from the heart and pen of Bonnie Evans, I at times felt transported to another time or place in my own life. Her writings have a way of taking you to moments in your life when, perhaps, questions still linger. Through the insights she shares with amazing transparency, I felt the courage to follow thoughts and memories down my own path to discover more of life's lessons. Thank you, Bonnie, for sharing yourself in the pages of this beautiful book."

—Jervae Brooks
Executive Director—International Field, Aglow International
Author of *A Battle For Destiny*

"I can't tell you how inspirational your book is to me. Every word written was meant for me; every feeling shared was a feeling I have felt. These words remind me that I am not the only one who goes through tough times."

—Debbie Holewinski

"I can relate to so much of what you've written. You jerked my heartstrings with some of the pieces. 'Foundations' brought the memories rolling in. I related to your work on several levels: personal, emotional, and spiritual."

—Carol Zogata

"I loved the photo inserts; they added to the articles and reminded me of God's creation and how beautiful He made our everyday lives. We just have to look!"

—Donna Liedtke

"A great reminder that God is always with us and that the best is yet to come."

—Nancy Berger

"I must have read it a dozen times and appreciate it more each time. You really have a gift and are using it well. It's something I would like to share with my kids; it really is connected to memories for me as I know it is for you. I feel like it has been a bridge to reconnect us after all these years and miles. Thank you for allowing me to be a part of this venture."

—Glenda Bursky

BLOOMING *in the* DARK

Hope for
Those Going
Through
Hard Times

For permission:
        http://www.BonnieEvansLegacies.com
        bonniere@gmail.com

ISBN 13: 978-0991563425
ISBN 10: 0991563425   Library of Congress Catalog Card Number: 2012913524

BLOOMING *in the* DARK

Hope for
Those Going
Through
Hard Times

BONNIE EVANS

Legacies,
Preserving memories of ordinary people
Pine Grove, California
http://www.BonnieEvansLegacies.com

This book is dedicated to those who helped me bloom in places I never asked to be planted. May you always remember how little it takes to keep another moving forward in the journey of life.

Contents

Foreword by Carolyn Suty

Only light can dispel or reveal what happens in the dark, and that's what happens in this powerful book of metaphors and testimonies. Bonnie, who has a spiritual light deep within, has peered into the darkness and given us hope for times when things look bleak.

I have known Bonnie over twenty years and watched as she walked through the situations described here; she came through each one with greater wisdom and understanding. Then she had the ability to reach deep within and (without judgment or pity) draw a map that brings us into a new place. As a resourceful teacher, she paints beautiful word pictures to expose her trials so we can dare to open up and reveal we struggle in that way too. Isn't that what life is all about? So many Christians and non-Christians today don't let their relationships go into a deeper place of intimacy and honesty. We need to be real, and bloom in fullness and freedom of life. *Blooming in the Dark* offers reality and honesty, and brings hope that we too will be able to make it.

Being transparent is difficult for most people. We work at looking and speaking like we have it all together. I love this book, for its honesty in the reality of life. *Blooming in the Dark* is a must read as we face trials and difficulties along the way. Thanks, Bonnie, for sharing your journey.

- Carolyn Suty
- U.S. Regional Director for Aglow International

Preface

God is everywhere and in everything that happens. He's even in the night and woven through our darkest moments. Of course, at least in my life, He doesn't usually arrive in a white robe or surrounded by lightning and fiery chariots. He shows up in the bloom of a flower long awaited, a fresh layer of snow, or a miraculous rescue. Knowing He is always with me gives me the courage to bloom wherever I am and in whatever conditions I'm temporarily planted.

Since I believe God comforts us in ALL our afflictions so we can comfort others in ANY affliction (2 Corinthians 1:3–5), I felt compelled to gather various ways God has wrapped me in His wonderful grace in the hope of encouraging others.

The following material is gleaned from a variety of things I've written over the last thirty-five years. It includes articles, journal entries, inspirational thoughts, editorial columns, poetry, and prayers. Since much of my God-given comfort and many of my well-earned lessons involve metaphors from nature, quite a few of the excerpts have natural settings. I love to listen to the trees whisper, watch a creek giggle wildly as it rushes on to parts unknown, or smell the sweet aroma of a wildflower. Those times soothe and broaden perspective far beyond a single day in my overspent life.

Some of the enclosed pieces started out as entries in my please-help-me-understand-this-moment journal ("Just When I Think," "Clouds," "Foundations," "Lord, I Want to Love You More," and "Dream's Journey"). Some of those reflections turned into blogs and garnered enough positive feedback to earn a place in this little book. One, "Dream's Journey," has never been allowed outside the gates of my journal before this small tome went to print. When I wrote this poem about a lost, long-held dream, it never occurred to me I'd someday bury enough dreams to fill a small private cemetery or dare to share those personal sorrows with others.

Another piece, "The Bear Family," was a writing assignment for a college course I took at the age of forty-five. The instructions were to write an extended metaphor using an animal as your primary symbol. When I read my essay to the class, two of the young women got teary-eyed. I hadn't been overly impressed with the piece and was startled by their response. How can you not set those words in a safe place until you figure out what to do with them?

Other pieces were written with the thought, *I hope an editor will like me enough to buy me* ("Blooming in the Dark," "Of Leeches and Fungi," "Surprised by Life," "Lost and Found," and "Journey of Hope"). Depending on the magazine I was submitting to, I wrote in the slant and style they preferred. You will no doubt sense those inclusions have a different tone than the ones written for an audience of one.

At one point in my life, I had the privilege of writing an editorial column for the *Gilroy Dispatch*, a daily newspaper in Gilroy, California. Mark Derry, the gracious editor and my boss, had five of us with varying political viewpoints writing on a specific day of the week. From time to time, I used that platform to address cultural issues from a religious perspective. Two of those pieces have been reworked and included in this book ("Jacob's Hug" and "The Best is Yet to Come").

My prayer is you'll find comfort and encouragement in this eclectic collection of words and photography. May it inspire you to bloom in your dark times and persuade you you're not alone no matter how dense the night or how bright the light. God will never leave you nor forsake you. Indeed, He has your name written on the palms of His hands and thoughts of you are ever before Him. Amen? Amen!

Acknowledgments

- I'd like to thank my parents, Dale and Doris Marquard, for raising me in a Christian home and sending me to Christian schools, choir, and confirmation. I'd also like to acknowledge their indirect funding of this project. When my father died in 1982, my mom gave me some money in his memory. I set it aside thinking someday something would come along needing special funding. This booklet was financed by that gift. Thanks Mom and Dad!

- I'd like to thank Mike Evans, my husband, who sometimes makes fun of how much time I spend at my computer trying to crank out words that make sense. In spite of the jokes, he always supports my adventures in writing as well as my passion for encouraging others. He really is the wind beneath my wings!

- I'd like to thank the women who helped proof and critique the manuscript. I emailed ten women in the hopes of finding two who had time to help me. Much to my delight, six said they would do what they could to see this project cross the finish line.

> Donna Liedtke, my favorite older sister
> Debbie Holewinski, my favorite little sister
> Glenda Bursky, my third sister (actually my second cousin)
> Nancy Berger, the bubbly lady married to my quietest cousin
> Carol Zogata, my cousin and Wild West Wyoming friend
> Marilynn Ludwig, my friend in Amador County paradise

- Lastly, I'd like to thank Bill Gothard, a man I've never met but whose wisdom continues to affect my life profoundly. He teaches that Christians without a clearly defined ministry should find a need and fill it. I've found this simple advice works wonderfully and is an awesome way to find fulfillment in life. There are so many things I know I can't do (either through lack of skill, opportunity, or funding), but when I ask for eyes to see the needs all around me and a heart willing to meet those needs, God answers every time.

The Evening Primrose

The Evening Primrose is an unusual flower that blooms in the night.

Any old flower can blossom in sunshine;
it takes a special one to open up
and flourish in the dark.

Blooming in the Dark

"Weeping may tarry for the night, but joy comes with the morning." Psalm 30:5

Evening Primrose blossoms don't last long (twelve hours if the day isn't a hot one), but their brief glory in the morning is well worth each short-lived bloom.[1]

Over a year and a half ago, nursery staff recommended Evening Primrose plants for my barren backyard. Their sales pitch promised a fast-growing plant whose delicate blooms opened during the night. Intrigued, I took a leap of faith and brought six plants home.

With pick and shovel I scratched a shallow grave in our hard clay soil and tamped special potting soil around each fragile base.

All through the summer I watered, waited, and watched.

Before the first snowflakes fell, my six plants had grown two whole inches and only one teased me with a bud that never bloomed! Discouraged, I stopped watching and walked away.

When spring arrived, I spent days clearing mulch, twigs, and fallen leaves from our garden beds. To my surprise, the bright leaves of four surviving primrose plants peeked through the loam. Out came the fertilizer, watering can, and hope.

The plants began to grow; they grew fast and big. They formed a wall that blocked our view. I pruned brutally. They grew even faster and bigger. Every time I saw their bushy wonder, I'd sigh and shake my head.

"If I don't get a flower soon," I promised my husband, "I'll move them to the side of the house where I could use some greenery."

Early one sunny morning two weeks later, I spotted a lone flower hiding in the leafy hedge. Her brow still wet with dew, she seemed to wink and ask for patience. I chose to heed her plea.

Daybreak three weeks later, six blossoms dressed in glorious apparel waited for my applause. I felt as if someone had transplanted joy into my unyielding yard while I lay dreaming and carefully braided its roots to the faith, hope, and patience already thriving there.

Sunup four weeks later found the bushes loaded with the uncommonly lovely blooms. My spirit soared. I snapped photos from every angle and sat staring for hours, savoring the sight.

By noon, the hot sun wilted their brightness; by dinner, they had collapsed into slack pods of beige.

"It was worth the wait to see them this morning," I said, thinking I'd waited a year and a half for this single explosion of yellow.

I was wrong.

Every sunrise since, I've witnessed the incredible mystery of flowers that bloom in the darkness and raise their radiant faces toward whatever the day might bring. Each time I see the display, I remember Jeremiah's words of expectation and praise, "But this I call to mind, and therefore I have hope: The steadfast love of the Lord never ceases, his mercies never come to an end; they are new every morning; great is thy faithfulness" (Lamentations 3:21–23).

Lord, help me practice patience when life is barren and no amount of diligence seems to bear fruit. Baptize me with the hope that defies understanding: I shall again see the goodness of the Lord in the land of the living. And, when you send joy unspeakable, remind me to take a picture with the shutters of my heart; may each day of breath and life be viewed through the memories of your undeserved grace and unmerited blessing. I am yours. Yours to plant, prune, and pluck. Amen.

Foundations

Even though I haven't lived there for forty years, I still call a trip to Wisconsin "going home." Last year duty invited me to lay a hand on my roots and the strength they lend to my heart. And so we drove 2,300 miles to sleep beneath the night calls of lake loons and fireflies blinking in the dark.

Myriad groves of lush forests still crowd the asphalt, cement, or in some cases, crushed red granite roads of this state in the middle of America the Beautiful. As the spring-bloomed trees lean over the byways in a thousand shades of green, a surreal sense threatens that if cars stop traveling beneath them on a regular basis they'll jump back onto the graded paths and make the roads disappear in a matter of weeks.

Here and there the thick woods cede space to a wedge of farm. A few of them are mega farms where I'm told the cows line themselves up on conveyor belts and milk themselves twice a day! But those aren't the farms that call my name with unrelenting sweetness. My eyes search for the old, two-story farmhouses set on a slight rise about a stone's throw from the animals and surrounded by an acre of cropped lawn. The cows (Guernsey, brown-and-white, and Holstein) chew their cud or wait anxiously by the barn door for the farmer to relieve them of their milky burdens.

I glance at animals and houses, but the barns imprison my stare. How weathered are their boards, how steep or rounded their roof, how many silos perch next to their aging walls, and is the milk house attached or separate? Some of the barns look new; their paint is bright and right-cut cement blocks hold up the walls. But I also see my favorites: antiques with graying boards and fieldstone foundations. That sight has the power to trigger one of my favorite childhood memories…

The sky is black at 4:30 a.m. when Uncle Wally calls up the attic stairwell where we snuggle three to a bed.

I hear his husky voice but know I don't have to get up like Glenda does. I'm company. I stretch legs into the warm space her body leaves and pull the quilt to my chin. Do I want to stay put or go? I imagine hunting for yesterday's cold clothes and my tennis-shoed feet crunching their way to the barn. Taking two steps down into the milking section, I'll be greeted by the sounds of cows munching oats, an occasional lowing, and the soft sucking of milk pumps. I'll see family staring nowhere in silence as they wait for the next chore. The sour smell of bovine urine mingled with the earthy scent of ground grains will tickle my nose and make me sneeze. Those predictable predawn pleasures spur me into clumping down the wooden steps minutes after my last cousin bangs the screen door.

We might have an hour or two to play later, I think as we hunker down in the barn's alleys. Maybe we'll play hide-and-seek in the cornfields, flatten sections of oats so we can lie down and dream big dreams for our little lives, listen to the hollow sound of our echoing voices in a half empty silo, or build houses out of bales of hay and pretend they're the elegant manors of rich people who have nothing to do but squander time and gossip.

At breakfast, I discover the day has an added chore and no allotted free time. The lower field needs to have the stones picked and all kids within shouting distance are invited to participate. Pick stones? We've picked and husked corn, made oats, and shucked peas—but how do you pick stones? Where do they grow and why do kids have to pluck them?

Jimmy laughs while Glenda explains. Over time, winter's ice pushes rocks to the surface of fields meant for crops. Every few years they have to be stripped of the accumulating stones or the plows will break or bend when the two connect.

It doesn't sound too hard.

Uncle Wally hitches a low wagon to his tractor and drives slowly up and down the furrowed rows. We children fan out behind it; if we spot a rock, we toss it onto the flatbed. Jimmy decides we should climb carefully onto the moving trailer one at a time and see if we can get to the end of the row without Uncle Wally knowing he's hauling kids not rocks! We never make it, but it's still fun because we spend the warm afternoon transforming work into play.

The rocks our hands lifted from those black, fertile fields? They were unceremoniously dumped in a pile down by the cow pond. When it was time to build a barn, milk house, fence, or anything else that needed to be held up, held out, or held in, they were used to form the sturdy foundation.

Those are the rock walls I watched for on my journey home. To me, they symbolize everything family stands for: laughing, crying, teasing, playing, dreaming, working, tearing down, lifting up, and building what needs to be built. They're memorials of time spent together and the substance of core values lying far beneath my skin. Their harnessed power holds all things to come—the good, the bad, and the ugly—in their proper place.

We left Wisconsin with hugs, urges to return soon, and sad farewells. Against a backdrop of whippoorwill cries, I heard the voices of those I love. "Don't wait so long to come back." "Be careful." "I love you." "I love you more." "I love you the mostest."

Those echoes are like a fresh coat of paint to well-weathered planks, girding poles to leaning walls, or shake tiles for a slumped ceiling. They sustain what's hidden beneath the sagging floorboards of the life called "Bonnie" and give me the strength to be home no matter where I am.

This photograph as well as that of the barn at the beginning of this article were taken by Glenda Bursky; she wrote: "I got some pictures of Julie's old barn and a little barn. The little one looks like it may have been the first house built when it was a homestead; it has rooms and windows and then a lower floor where livestock was kept. No one remembers it as anything but a chicken coop and pig barn, but the upstairs has rooms and doors and a chimney for a cook stove as well as windows and finished walls, so I am invoking poetic license and calling it a home."

*These pictures were taken by Nancy Berger
from the area surrounding Mosinee,
Wisconsin.*

When Life Gets Hard

When life gets hard,
find something soft to hold.

*"I have calmed and quieted my soul, like a child quieted at its
mother's breast; like a child that is quieted is my soul."*
Psalm 131:2

Unconditional Love in Full Bloom

The rose symbolizes the enduring and unconditional spirit of love.

May love grow and grow until it reaches full bloom in my heart. Amen.

"Do you love me more than these?"

[Jesus to Peter after his death and resurrection. John 21:15 MSG]

Lord, I Want to Love You More

Lord, I love you but I want to love you more.

More than husband and children,
More than family or friends,
More than I love myself,
More.

More than pride,
More than resentment and unforgiveness,
More than I hate my enemies,
More.

More than secret sins,
More than fear, shame, or shyness,
More than my needs and all of my wants,
More than comfort, safety, or happiness,
More.

Yes, Lord, above all else,
I want to love you more than these,
I want to love you more.

Just When I Think...

For I, the Lord your God, hold your right hand;
it is I who say to you, 'Fear not, I will help you.'" Isaiah 41:13

Just when I think God has delivered all the good and perfect gifts I'm scheduled to receive this side of paradise, someone in heaven gets the idea that—when the temperature is just right and winter has need of something more than cold water sloshing down to meet minimal rainfall quotas—droplets should slightly freeze and puff up into untraceable, unrepeatable shapes.

And, instead of cascading down in dreary transparent rhythms, the fluff should turn white, hold hands, and flutter down like regal queens on their way to an elegant ball. And then, instead of sinking quickly into the thirsty earth, the debutantes linger quietly as if primly waiting for Prince Charming to ask their hand in dance.

Sometimes that visual present arrives during the night and I wake up to a world cloaked in a soft, pearlescent mantle. Bare trees hold inches of beauty on each tiny twig and every lofty branch; their darkness transformed by the grace they didn't expect and certainly don't deserve. Pine trees droop, heavily laden with the exquisite signs of God's artistic finger.

Silence reigns as if even the air has bowed in honor of the descended glory.
It's a quiet unbroken by plumes of breath, bird songs, or deer ambling along forest paths.
A stillness that hushes hearts and muffles even the heaviest worry.

And then, just when I think God's done quite enough for the day—
it'll already take me the better part of the morning to let this tapestry of love
touch my deepest needs—He chooses to do even more.

He pulls back the darkened clouds and releases the sun to race down,
kneel, and kiss each flocked item with prisms of light and joy.
The pristine display awakens inner tears and swelling hymns of praise,
Oh Lord my God, how great thou art, how great thou art!

I've noticed I'm often surprised like this just when I've begun to wonder
if I'll be able to hang on until the first green bud slips out in spring.
Just when I've begun to wonder if the rain will ever stop and if the sky is really blue.
Just when I've begun to think the bare bones of disappointment and hurt
will never release me or those I love.

Those are the times God decides to stay up all
night to fashion a faith-renewing miracle for my
barren heart. This time I think He smiled with
pleasure over the package He sent while I lay
sleeping. Because just this time,
He chose to spell hope:

S-N-O-W.

Of Leeches and Fungi: Relationship Metaphors from Nature

If possible, so far as it depends upon you, live peaceably with all." Romans 12:18

No sane adult would have entered the blooming Wisconsin lake, but my sisters and I never noticed the color or less-than-fresh smell. We only saw a chance to rinse off the sticky June heat and waded quickly into the world of make-believe.[2]

We pulled lily pads and wore them on our heads like crowns. We built castles out of stones the winter ice had pushed onto our beach. We floated doll-sized birch canoes across our newly dug moats.

By the time the sultry sun slipped below the horizon, we were sunburned and hungry. I carefully patted my baked body with a faded Minnie Mouse towel. As my wrinkled feet slipped into worn blue flip-flops, I noticed some strange brown clumps between my toes. I bent down and pushed one with a fingernail. They squirmed but didn't brush off. *Hey wait a minute, they're ALIVE!*

My sisters squealed and assessed their own shriveled limbs to see if they had a moving collection of slimy somethings. They did not. Mom was not the least bit shocked at the sight of my unwelcome guests.

"They're leeches," she quipped.

"What're leeches?"

"They live in lake mud. If you stand still too long, they grab on and suck your blood."

"Take 'um off! I don't want 'um on my feet! Take 'um off!"

Mom calmly reached for the saltshaker and shook a generous portion on my sad little feet. The leeches curled and slid onto the hot sand without a struggle.

That's the last time I stood still too long in a spring-fed lake, but it's not the last time I thought about the lessons learned. Whenever I find myself mired in the stagnant, muddied waters of an unhealthy relationship, I remember that every so often people resemble lake leeches and that sometimes they even call themselves friends.

Figurative bloodsuckers are those who never learned the ebb and flow of a healthy friendship. In their world, there are Givers and Takers, and the Takers get to take even when the Givers aren't giving. Occasionally these lopsided interactions are even encouraged under the false guise of Christian virtues (compassion, humility, support, or service).

I confess I find myself in these uncomfortable liaisons often (which may say as much about me as it about does the parasites I host). They usually leave me feeling drained, used, manipulated, and eventually, depressed.

My doctor was the first to point out the correlation between usurpers and their target's sense of well-being. I went to see her because I'd been blue for months and thought the cause might be medical. When the tests returned normal, she suggested I start an emotional chart.

"Log each hour, what you did, who you were with, what you ate or drank, and then grade how you felt," she instructed. "Did the activities affect your mood positively or negatively?"

Eager to avoid medication, I complied.

Within two weeks, patterns emerged. After every phone call or one-on-one meeting with the Takers in my life, I saw my mood lines dip dramatically. The chart proved Takers lured me into feeling resentment, anger, hurt, and depression. I'd been denying those feelings because I couldn't reconcile them with my Christianity, but now it was time to do a little circle-of-friends housecleaning. At once. Not necessarily an easy task, but one that bore hope.

A stone's throw from those same Wisconsin lakes, nature displays another kind of relationship, this one mutually beneficial…

Deep beneath the rich black floor of the forest, a mycorrhizal fungus moves into the root systems of a conifer tree. At first glance, this appears to be another parasite/host association, but it's not. The fungus, isolated from streams of sunlight, cannot carry out the life-giving process of photosynthesis, so it takes the sugars it needs from the pine roots. In return, the fungus provides the tree with antibiotics against parasites and pathogens as well as supplying water, nutrients, and oxygen from the soil.

In nature, reciprocal associations are fairly common; among humanity, rare.

Carol is from my limited edition of symbiotic friends and I'm grateful God introduced us many years ago.

In appearance, we're as different as the pine tree and fungi: She's almost six feet tall with long thin legs; I'm five feet four inches and quite round. She has dark hair, dark eyes, and olive skin; I'm blonde, blue-eyed, and freckle when I'm in the sun too long. Our differences don't end on the surface either: our personalities and opinions are worlds apart.

Our friendship began when we became walking partners. We must have been quite a sight charging down the levee for our daily trek: Carol wearing two sets of ankle weights to slow her down; my short legs pumping wildly to maintain the gait of my hobbled victim. We walked, we talked, we laughed, we listened, we cried. We puffed and panted and sweated and strained. Conceived in an excuse to exercise, pregnant with a mutual yearning for fellowship, laboring from our differences, the miracle of closeness came.

I find verbal sparring with Carol exhilarating and stimulating. So far, we haven't resolved any of our arguments, but the discussions continue to inspire reflection, prayer, and Bible study.

Carol calls when she doesn't need anything; sometimes I'm compelled to send her an outrageous Shoebox greeting card for no apparent reason. When we go somewhere, we take turns driving. If we stop for lunch, we split the bill.

It's refreshing to know I have a friend who can handle me on my down days. She doesn't demand composure by downplaying dilemmas. She listens, affirms, and accepts. I'm comfortable telling her how much I hate it when she's late (which is often). The comfort comes from knowing my flaws might just as easily earn comments. Privately.

God challenges me to grow in character and grace when I bond with either the fungi or the leeches in my life; however, I've learned to watch for those times when I'm mired in the muck more than I'm walking in the woods.

I've gotten quicker at spotting friendships that consistently bring more pain than pleasure and quicker at taking action. When I've grown sufficiently tired of the way they leave me feeling, I ask God to please liberally sprinkle some salt on my tired heart or at least show me where the shaker is so I can reach for it myself.

Signs you might need to ask God to pass the salt:
You have a friend who...

- only calls when they need something
- never shares in mutual expenses
- likes sympathy and compassion but rarely gives it
- talks more than they listen
- doesn't like it when you're down
- doesn't like it when you disagree with them
- consistently leaves you feeling guilty, used, down, depressed

Ways to shake salt on an unbalanced friendship:
♥ ask God to show you your part in the lopsided interaction
♥ humble yourself, the relationship didn't get out of whack without your help
♥ ask God for a scripture that shows you how to pray for yourself
♥ ask God for a scripture that shows you how to pray for the other person
♥ ask God if you should work on the friendship or if you should sever the tie
♥ if you feel God wants you to share, first take responsibility for your actions
♥ then invite them to share how they feel about the relationship
♥ pray with them and ask God to bless them

Clouds

The sky is blue,
a periwinkle hue.
Its pure color guards the day
from querulous weather
planning to spoil our play.
Everyone agrees unfettered rays
are what we need for just-sowed seeds
and long summer days.

My lips agree but my heart gives pause,
it's not sure how to express the thought:
Clouds make the sky prettier still
when they float and wander high and at will.
They break the boredom of a solo shade
into shapes that twist, swell, and slowly fade.

The massive ones draw my gaze the most,
darker than dark but rimmed with light,
they whisper "the sun shines somewhere
even when its glory is out of sight."
They promise showers
and cool air, washed clean by rain;
ruined hairdos and muddy shoes
guarantee my garden's gain.

Skies without clouds are like life without pain,
without sorrow, sadness, trauma, or shame.
Everyone thinks that's the way it should be
and that sapphire is all we should see;
but my soul whispers it's the clouds of life—
framed in hope but seeded with strife—
that lift joy higher and make it brighter,
sink peace deeper and make it last,
strengthen laughter,
keep knees bent, and praises sent:
"This too is the day that the Lord has planned,
I WILL rejoice with the gift at hand."

Jacob's Hug

They say "a picture is worth a thousand words," but I've never been too eager to have mine taken. Whenever possible, I'm holding the camera, or the short person in the back row slouching behind the heads of others.[3]

There was, however, a time in my life when no amount of aw-shucks ducking kept me out of the camera's eye, and it couldn't have come at a worse time. I was writing a column for the local newspaper and the editor decided the column needed a mug shot to go with my weekly allotted words.

I stalled as long as I could and then made an appointment with the persistent editor to justify my reticence. Wearing the wig that looked just like my long-gone puffy blonde hair, I explained, "I just finished my sixth cycle of chemotherapy, I'm bald and have the swollen moon face that comes from massive doses of steroids. I can't bear the thought of having a current picture published in the paper. Could I just submit a black-and-white taken before I got sick?"

The editor graciously agreed even though the offered photo was a few years behind the times. Almost as soon as it ran, I started getting emails and phone calls from friends and family.

"That photo doesn't look anything like you," was the common chorused tease.

"That's the point!" I'd glibly respond, feeling perfectly confident it didn't matter what the picture or "I" looked like; the important thing was a chance to spend 750 words on a timely topic.

During those same hairless hard times, someone else extended some much-needed grace; and, even though he was only five when it happened, he reinforced the lesson that it's not how we look or what we say, but who we are that counts. His name was Jacob and he was a kindergartener at a school where I subbed often.

Months after my last chemo treatment, my hair had only grown one inch. (Yes, I measured it. Once a day. With a ruler.) And, no matter how much goo or hair spray I used, cowlicks kept the dark fuzz going any which way but nice. I was miserable under my wig, it itched and made me sweat, but I couldn't stand myself without it.

Come June, during one triple-digit week of heat, I was scheduled to return to Jacob's class. It would be too hot to wear my fake hair, and as much as I dreaded the thought, I knew it was time to start going au naturel.

Looking at my crew cut in the mirror one more time before I opened the classroom door, I mentally braced myself for the honesty of kindergarteners.

Though most just stared with silent disbelief as if trying to decide if I was who I used to be, one little girl whispered to her friend, "Mrs. Evans looks ri-diiiiiiiii-cu-lous!"

I smiled and nodded; all too true.

By the time the first bell rang, the kids had forgotten I no longer looked like myself and so had I. There was work to do and, as always, we would have fun doing it together.

After opening with the kindergarten calendar-routine, I gave instructions for making Father's Day cards and walked around to help as needed.

"Mrs. Evans, you got your hair cut," Jacob said when I got to his table.

"Yes, Jacob," I fibbed, not wanting to say that medicine made it fall out.

"Ya know, it's very short," he said as he cut out a polka-dot tie.

"Yes, I know. It's very, Very, VERY short!"

"Ya know," he stopped cutting to look up at me, "ya kinda look like a boy."

I smiled and met his worried eyes. "I know, Jacob, but it'll grow." Reaching up and pretending to pull on the ends of my dark stubble, I said, "Every night before I go to bed, I tell it to pleeeeeeeease grow before morning. But when I wake up, it still looks like this."

The children looked up, giggled at my pantomime, and then returned to their work.

Jacob was the last to finish his card.

"I'm glad you took your time printing," I complimented him. "I love the picture of you and your dad playing catch!"

Beaming, he put the card in his cubby and started toward some children building a house out of wooden blocks. All of a sudden, he stopped and turned to look at me. I could feel a pair of wise brown eyes in a little boy face probing carefully beneath my practiced smile. After a couple of seconds, they seemed to spot a need that was just his size.

Without a word, he came and threw both arms around my knees and squeezed with every ounce of strength a child could muster. Just as suddenly, he let go and went to play. The incident lasted less than a minute, yet the simple act of kindness left its fingerprints on my heart forever.

I had many more good and bad days in the following wigless weeks. Eventually I stopped measuring my hair and explaining why I had none.

When my inner strength failed, I'd take a deep breath and remember how it felt to have Jacob's hug wrapped around my weak knees. A child had seen beneath the surface and affirmed what lay beneath.

Jacob was right. I'm more than my hair, wrinkle count, or wardrobe. I'm more than a photograph and even more than my wisest words. What gives me value is the treasure God has hidden within. That amazing fact serves as a constant reminder that the transcendent power belongs to Him and not me.

Gardenia,
flower of grace and beauty

Tulipmania

Did you know in the years 1636–37, "tulipmania" ruled in the Netherlands?
Tulips were a symbol of wealth and status and were traded like currency.
A bed of tulips could buy a small house.

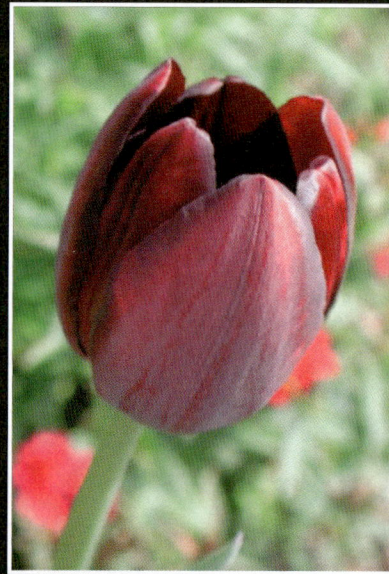

"Has anyone by fussing before the mirror ever gotten taller by so much as an inch? If fussing can't even do that, why fuss at all? Walk into the fields and look at the wildflowers. They don't fuss with their appearance—but have you ever seen color and design quite like it?

The ten best-dressed men and women in the country look shabby alongside them. If God gives such attention to the wildflowers, most of them never even seen, don't you think he'll attend to you, take pride in you, do his best for you?"

—Luke 12:25–28 (MSG)

False Spring, False Hope

"Why are you down in the dumps, dear soul? Why are you crying the blues? Fix my eyes on God—soon I'll be praising again. He puts a smile on my face. He's my God."
Psalm 42:11 (MSG)

The wet but mild winter tricked my daffodils into rising early and blooming before their time. Lured by sunny days and tepid nights, the peach tree sprouted and loosed her bright pink blossoms ahead of schedule too. The dormant lawn went from sage brown to green almost overnight. Glad to see bright colors amidst the gray winter skies, I rejoiced at the premature signs of spring.

Then winter made a U-turn. March roared in with dark clouds, wild winds, low temperatures, and snow. Lots of snow. Tumbling wildly and blowing fiercely, the icy flakes buried the green, yellow, and pink colors of spring. Would the flowers survive their frozen grave? Could the peach blossoms hang on to the slender limbs where they were conceived? Would the lawn need to be reseeded?

Turning out the evening lights, my spirit sagged against the fickle hand of weather and how it changed my view.

Morning came dressed in arctic white. Usually on days like this I'm outside in bathrobe and slippers photographing the wonderland from every angle. This day was decidedly different.

Around noon, despite best intentions to keep my gaze averted, I happened to notice touches of yellow poking through the snowbanks. *What was this? Had the blooming flowers survived the frozen downpour?*

Slipping into garden clogs, I big-stepped my way to the ring of bulbs planted years ago. Sure enough, lying just beneath the surface, three daffodils begged to be released from their snowy captors. With fingertip, I urged the stems to rise and watched the blooms bob into the chilly air.

Their resilience made me smile and triggered a phrase waltzing through my head: *False spring, false hope.* Even after I'd gone back to chores, those words echoed until I whispered, "God, are you trying to tell me something?"

With little waiting, heaven replied. I was reminded of the free advertising I received last month and how it made hope bubble for my floundering business. A radio interview, an opportunity to speak, and a free blurb in the newspaper simultaneously unleashed a flood of optimism. The trio of opportunities implied the dry season was over, a corner was about to be turned, and blessings were heading in my direction. Spring had sprung.

By the end of the month, that buoyancy had deflated. None of the leads brought customers. Instead of being busy and rich, I was idle and poor. I'd foolishly planted hope in marketing strategies and stood by helplessly when it grew no roots and bore no fruit.

How many years has it been since I first confused faith with wishful thinking? How long since I learned God's wisdom is a kingdom far removed from the ways of the world? Or, that my expectancy is not to be placed in the care of someone, something, or someday but anchored in the only One with the power to perform the impossible?

Lord, it's not time to give up, it's time to go on. Go on with you! Put forth your right hand and urge my slumping spirit to soar over this moment. My life is yours to keep and spend in any way you choose. May it bear good fruit in its season. Amen.

The Flower of Hope

Daffodils are often considered the "flowers of hope."
A bouquet of these early spring bloomers is said to
lift the spirit of those struggling against disease,
in particular, those facing any type of cancer.

The Bear Family

Memories tend to warp when caught in the passing wake of time. Even if mine were sharper and more focused, I'd have to admit my father never gave a clearly defined reflection; the ones he did offer seemed to change with my age. But, no matter what year it was or how fair my vision, he always appeared to belong more to the family of Ursidae than ours.

When I was little, he seemed like a grizzly. Grizzlies shake their heads, rise tall on hind legs, and inspire terror in all small creatures. I usually kept a wise and healthy distance from the strange beast called Father during those years. On occasion, I'd carelessly wander into his unmarked domain. Then, enveloped in timidity, I'd inch away before finding out what his paws could do or the powerful jaws would say.

Sometime in my teens, I grew taller and he transfigured into a new kind of fear. Because he worked two jobs, he was rarely seen during daylight hours. No matter how rare the sightings, he always knew exactly what his cubs were up to and if they needed corrective action. Could it be he raked through his family's trailings like a black bear at the dump? Or perhaps he peered through darkened windows as we lay sleeping.

Right before I married and moved far out of his territory, a strange event indicated yet one more transformation. My assigned Saturday chore was to clean the cupboard below the china cabinet. During the course of that task, I found a black scrapbook filled with poetry. Tiny neat letters marched across every line on every page. One ode painted a powerful image of horses pulling a milk wagon in the dead of winter. My inside eyes could see their breath zagging into the gray, snowy sky. A signature scrawled at the bottom left corner spelled a name I recognized. His. Feeling I had seen a teddy bear without his fur, I closed and returned the book to its secret place beneath folded doilies and pressed tablecloths.

We know cave bears once roamed the earth because we see their skeletons scarred in fossilized rocks. The vague imprinted images don't tell us much, but they leave proof these enormous animals once lived as long and as well as they could.

My dad has been gone for quite a few years now. He died young and long before I could find the man inside his various bear disguises. Sometimes, I try to decipher the fuzzy legends of the grizzly, black bear, and teddy. When those spots of time come, I dream of pulling out the only rock etched with the way Dad saw things and tracing my finger over the curve of his words. Since the book with its compelling images no longer exists, prayers for understanding ascend.[4]

Occasionally my faith is rewarded with glimpses of things my childhood eyes could not see: a man who worked multiple jobs so his daughters could have things he never did; a man who sat with his family in church every Sunday; and a man who came dressed in khakis to watch his middle daughter lead the cheer squad, his shy smile spreading until it bloomed into full-fledged pride. Those are the reflections I choose to cling to, the ones that cradle my heart with his unseen hand.

Lord, *teach me to see what's really there and not what seems to be. Help me to know you as you really are and not through the haze of my fears. Guide me to the words you wrote and show me a clear image of just how much you love me. Amen.*

Dad as a boy with Babe and Beauty.

Dad with Donna and me one Easter morning long ago.

Journey of Hope

I've never been fond of birds, but today their sweet songs blessed me.[5]

I've never really liked the rain either, but today multitudes of raindrops gathered below the levee to glorify God, and I yearned to worship along with creation's joyful congregation.

Wanting to draw closer to the source, I left the gravel path and made my way down toward the fast-flowing creek and nature's music. Down. Down to the healing sounds.

The warming earth smelled like a farmer's plowed field. Slender shafts of grass tickled my legs and left them wet. A mossy rock invited me to rest for a while and remember how this journey started.

The nightmare began a year ago with flash floods of fatigue. It buckled my knees, sent me sprawling, made my arms too weak to put plates in the cupboard, and had me in bed early. I assumed it was from my compulsion for over-commitment and a bad season of allergies.

Slow down, I told myself. *Get more rest.*

The admonitions didn't help. Instead, things got worse: double vision, breathing spells, and fingers that no longer worked. Within weeks, the paresis in my hands had traveled up both arms and into my neck.

"No," I explained to the doctor, "my hands aren't numb; they just don't do what I tell them. I start typing, and pretty soon my fingers are wooden sticks slapping at the keyboard."

My doctor ran tests. The symptoms spread while each result came back negative. He hoped they would leave as suddenly as they had come. So did I. They didn't.

I dropped out of graduate school, resigned from volunteer posts, and quit working. I could no longer dress myself, drive a car, or walk unassisted. On a good day, I could say a couple of sentences before my tongue froze and my lungs ran out of air. On a bad day, I could say a couple of words before the muteness settled in.

Two days before Christmas, a neurologist pinpointed the presence of Myasthenia Gravis, an autoimmune disease that disrupts the communication between nerves and muscles.

"There is no cure," he spoke slowly as if to make the words kinder, "but often patients go into remission or find enough stability through medication to lead fairly normal lives. People don't die from it; they learn to live with it."

I tried to listen, but thoughts of my plans since the kids left for college—finishing my educational goals, having a career, contributing to the household budget—disintegrated in painful flashes.

"We'll do our best …" the doctor's promise droned on.

I don't want your best. My best is gone.

Traffic moved slowly on the ride home as walls of despair grew brick by bitter brick.

"All the king's horses and all the king's men couldn't put this Humpty Dumpty together again," I said to my chauffeur husband.

"Maybe all the king's horses and men can't," Mike answered after a few minutes of silence, "but the King can. Doctors don't have the power to give you your life back, God does. You just have to keep making choices that keep your feet on the path of hope."

I listened but didn't believe.

"It has now rained for sixty-one days straight," the weatherman reported last night on the news. "It's been the longest, wettest winter in one hundred years."

During that dark season, I visited doctors, physical therapists, chiropractors, and vitamin specialists. I had surgery, exercised weak limbs, took ninety-three vitamins and pills a day, and prayed.

Progress, so minute it was easy to miss, began to unfold. I could hold a toothbrush with one hand. Get out of the shower without help. Dress myself.

Most honest testimonies include a confession; this one does too. In the beginning I spent my days on the couch whining about the boredom and the silence. I grumbled about all I had lost and how lonely I felt. But somewhere during my journey of hope, I became accustomed to the new, calmer lifestyle and grateful for its quietness. God's presence had never been so real.

Bible verses became more than black words on a white page; they became His voice, the voice of a friend. No matter how isolated I felt, I knew I was never alone.

My complaints were replaced by an attitude of contentment and quiet thanksgiving. I found myself praising God for the simple things in life (the things I used to take for granted).

I was filled with awe that God could use physical weakness to spiritually strengthen me. Peace about my life having a purpose appeared from nowhere and grew. Jeremiah was right: God's compassions never fail, they're new every morning (paraphrased from Lamentations 3:22, 23).

On the sixty-second day of that exceedingly dreary winter, slivers of sunshine peeked through the black clouds and sent rainbows racing toward the horizon. For the first time in many months, I felt strong enough to go for a walk. Alone. What a sense of victory! Freedom!

I pushed off the rock's damp edge and continued down. Down the winding path. Cautiously down until I stood in silence at my very own Moriah.

"My plans are gone," I whispered to raindrops rushing out of sight.

"I know the plans I have for you," started the voice from somewhere in a corner of my heart, "plans for welfare and not for evil" (Jeremiah 29:11).

I stayed at the water's edge until truth had carried away each drop of disappointment. Until I resolved to trust God even if I couldn't understand Him, see His plan, or find its glory.

I was glad to be alive. I wasn't "doing" like I used to do, but I was "being" like I had never been.

When I got what I came down to get, I climbed ever so slowly and carefully up. Up. Up to where I started. The path looked the same, the sky looked the same, the day looked the same, I may have looked the same too, but I most certainly was not.

The Levee path in Gilroy, California. This photo was taken before the Army Corps of Engineers built a berm along the creek to keep it from flooding in the winter. They added a lovely, blacktopped walking path on the top of the berm for residents to walk, jog, and bike.

The Twelfth Day

"Blessed be the God and Father of our Lord Jesus Christ, the Father of mercies and God of all comfort, who comforts us in all our affliction, so that we may be able to comfort those who are in any affliction..."
2 Corinthians 1:3-4

It was Thanksgiving but I wasn't feeling very grateful. I still had long weeks to wait before my doctor finished reviewing all of the tests, pronounced a diagnosis, and suggested a cure. Would it be a brain tumor, Multiple Sclerosis, or Lupus? Or, would the results be inconclusive and send me to a new crew of specialists with a slew of different, painful medical procedures to endure?[6]

"How can you stand not knowing?" my sister asked from a state 2,000 miles away.

"I can't!" I answered trying unsuccessfully to stay calm. "Some of the tests are worse than the symptoms. But the waiting. . . . .the waiting is a nightmare! I hate to wake up in the morning and have to force myself to get out of bed."

Several days after that tearful conversation, a large box arrived for me via UPS. Inside I found a dozen numbered packages and a card from my sister instructing me to, "Open one gift each morning until your doctor's appointment."

I couldn't wait to open Surprise Number One. It was an Anne Geddes calendar for the next year—the attached note came with the admonition to "make plans for a future."

After adding doctor appointments, tests, and procedures to my brand new, beautiful calendar, I entered a couple of lunch dates and outings for June. It felt good to look ahead, to believe I'd be here in six months or be well enough to do something fun.

"I wonder what tomorrow's gift will be," I laughed as I showed my husband the calendar.

Each day now dawned with a clever, thoughtful treasure. There was a cute ornament for the Christmas tree I hadn't planned to put up but now *had to* because there was a new decoration for it. There was a twenty dollar bill with instructions to, "Buy fresh flowers and think about spring." There was a garden gnome for next summer's seeds, seedlings, blossoms, and fruit.

Each gift gave me something to look forward to and made me feel loved—the messages tucked inside inspired smiles and optimism. Though different sizes and shapes, they all made a powerful difference in a very difficult time. Conceived with care, they gave birth to hope.

Finally the day of the consult came. The doctor delivered hard news in a soft, kind voice: medication might help but there was no cure.

The words didn't hurt as much as they would have weeks ago. I had already begun to make plans for a future that might or might not include healing, might or might not include strength, might or might not include pain. My feet had found sure footing on a positive path and medical prophecies didn't have the strength to transform the scenery.

Lord, help me to be aware of those around me who are struggling and in need of encouragement. Give me creative ideas to meet the needs of their heart and turn their face toward hope. And then, give me the perseverance to follow through. Amen.

The Best is Yet to Come

The FedEx driver handed me the official-looking invitation, but I had a hard time comprehending its message.[7]

> *Congratulations! You have been selected as a Torchbearer for the Salt Lake 2002 Olympic Torch Relay. The public was asked to nominate someone they found inspirational to carry the Olympic Flame. You were nominated and I would like to personally invite you to carry the Olympic Flame as it travels across the landscape of America.*

I reread the letter and leafed through the packet of information for answers. Why me? Who had nominated me? What had I done to deserve it?

Though flattered by the idea, I didn't see myself accepting the request and began to compose a thanks-but-no-thanks letter. I know most athletic, work-out types fantasize about this sort of chance; but, I've always had, shall we say, a fluffy body. What would people think if they saw someone like me carrying a symbol of athletic excellence? Would they know I'd been nominated for "inspiring others" and not for physical prowess?

Mike was stranded in Wisconsin during the twenty-four hours I was given to respond, so I talked to Patti Anne, a close friend, about the invite and my plan to decline. She read the letter, cried, and said she thought it was God who had opened the door.

"You have to do it," she urged, "if not for yourself, for all those who have muscle disorders, chronic pain, or serious illnesses. For those who'll never be able to step on a treadmill or lift a weight or run a race. Carry the torch for them."

Her passionate speech elicited a new response: reluctant acceptance. I would face my fears and accept the challenge. I would do it for people like me: those who look normal but live with incurable, limiting diseases. Some who watched me would not understand; those who needed to, would.

Carrying the 2002 Olympic Torch for two-tenths of a mile was the hardest yet most exhilarating journey I've ever taken.

The torch is almost a yard long and weighs three and a half pounds. That may not seem like much to most folks, but I have Myasthenia Gravis, an autoimmune muscle disorder. As soon as they put it in my hands, I wondered if I'd be able to finish what I'd been invited to do.

Our Olympic hostess explained that the top five inches of the torch is made of crystal so people can see the fire as well as the fire mechanism. The next two-thirds is rough burnished steel sculptured in the form of fire racing uphill, which represents the past. The bottom third is smooth polished silver and has the 2002 Olympic theme inscribed on it—Light the fire within—this represented the future. We were to hold the torch where the past and the future meet because that's the present.

She closed by saying, "You've been nominated because you inspired others while going through adversity. This torch symbolizes your rough days are behind you and the best is yet to come."

Scottsdale, Arizona, where I was to partake in the event, had a huge turnout for the Torch Relay. Picture it: a pomp and circumstance parade with the spotlights shining on one person, the person carrying the torch. For two-tenths of a mile, that person was me.

Crowds cheered, waved flags, smiled, asked for my autograph, and cried. It was overwhelming. I've never really liked all-eyes-on-me kinds of activities; I'm more of a paint-me-wallpaper kind of person. But, this somehow felt right.

I did well until the point in my walk where large bushes kept spectators from lining the street. I kept switching arms but neither seemed to have enough strength to keep the jet-fueled fire hoisted into the night sky.

I remembered our instructions, "Support runners are right behind you. If you can't finish, pass the torch to them and they'll carry it on your behalf."

Not wanting to drop my precious cargo, I thought: *I had my fifteen seconds in the sun, there's no shame in asking for help.*

Just as I'd convinced myself to quit prematurely, I heard a voice calling from somewhere close, "Bonnie, you're almost there. I'm right behind you."

I turned to look. There was my seventy-three-year-old mother running along the side of the street, believing I could finish.

Just knowing the end was near and that someone who knew my name was with me infused miraculous strength into me. I did what I came to do.

Why did God give me this once-in-a-lifetime opportunity? I may never know all of His reasons, but I've recognized a few. Out of the richness of His wisdom, He taught me lessons about the supernatural power of encouragement. Under the umbrella of His watchful eye, He commissioned a weak person to bear a heavy burden and then gave her the strength to do it. From His amazing and abundant grace, He chose to honor me while others watched.

In addition to the spiritual blessings, I have many other reminders of this humbling, life changing experience. Thanks to my personal entourage of twenty-three family members, I have twenty-five rolls of film, two video clips, scraps, maps, memorabilia, notes, words, and letters of the event. I have the torch I carried sitting in my office in a stand with my name and the date I carried it engraved on its precious side.

Every time I look at or touch one of the items associated with that day, I'm reminded of the trek. I'm reminded of people who love me and believe I can do impossible things. And, most importantly, I'm reminded that the best is yet to come.

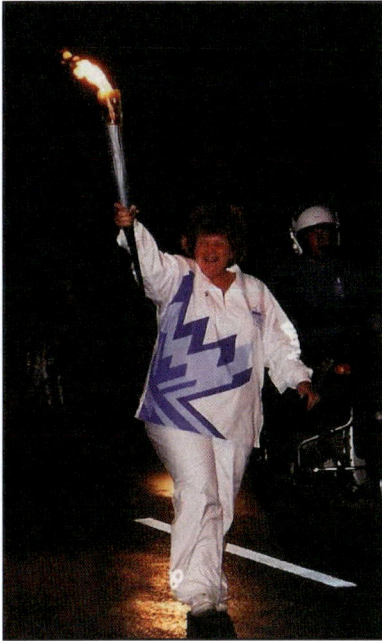

January 13, 2002

Left: *Scottsdale, Arizona*

Below, left-to-right:
> *Debbie Holewinski, my younger sister*
> *My mom, Doris Marquard*
> *Me*
> *Donna Liedtke, my oldest sister and the one who began the letter writing campaign to get me nominated*

The Glory

Lord, just once I wish you'd ask me to do something
I can kinda sorta do.

With a hint of heaven chuckling, He replied,
"If you could do it on your own, you wouldn't need me.
This way, if something good comes out of your obedience,
we'll both know who deserves the glory."

Solid Ground

It took the motor coach hours to get to the mouth of the Tutshi River where gold miners built boats to carry them the last 500 miles to the Yukon. We were there to walk across the new suspension bridge, but my love of history insisted I stop to read all the historical markers rimming the gravel pathway.

My lollygagging meant the busload of tourists I'd traveled with had already trekked across the very long, very high, very precarious suspension footbridge before I got to its gate. It meant I'd have to go across alone.

I stepped carefully onto the swinging pathway. Not even forty paces into my cautious journey, I chanced to look toward the hills birthing the avalanche of surging water far beneath my feet. The sun peeked through the overcast sky for the first time that day and silhouetted the purple and green flocked hills. It made the riotous water appear as if it was carrying diamonds to some point beyond the bend.

I need a picture of this. My fear-stiffened fingers left the side rails so I could slip out my camera and take one shot upstream and one down. As soon as the camera was safely secured into its case, I grabbed the chain-link ropes and finished crossing.

My cohorts cheered as my first foot touched solid ground.

"I can't believe you walked it by yourself," one lady said. "I almost didn't come across when I saw how much this thing moves and how far down it is."

Soon it was time to re-cross the bridge.

Since I was the last to arrive, I was the last to return. It was far different than my solo foray earlier. Forty-some bodies chugged to the other side in random rhythms. To make matters worse, one of the men thought it was funny to clomp and sway so the whole bridge rocked and rolled like a pedestrian roller coaster. Amidst the shouts of others for him to stop, I was hit with a cruel flood of paralyzing fear. Vertigo replaced the beauty, sunshine, and pleasure I'd owned just moments before. I froze physically, emotionally, and mentally.

I can't move, but I have to get across. How do I make that happen?

I saw my compadres reach the other side and climb steps to the roadway. How I wished that were me, heading for my seat on the bus. It also gave me an idea. If I didn't think about where I was but focused on where I wanted to be, perhaps I could will my feet to move.

It worked. Inch by inch, foot by foot, hand chink to hand chink, I moved closer and closer to my goal.

Finally air was replaced by soil and I breathed a silent sigh of relief. I boarded the bus with a permafrost smile on my face and my heart still thudding in its cage. Fortunately, those who had celebrated my triumphant journey forward didn't seem to notice my cowardly trip back.

***Lord**, when I feel frozen in fear, sure I cannot do what lies before me, help me set my forehead like flint and assure me I shall not be put to shame. Put a path of faith beneath my faltering feet so I may walk boldly toward the goal and be satisfied. Give me the grace to enjoy the journey no matter how bumpy the ride. Amen.* (Isaiah 50:7 paraphrased)

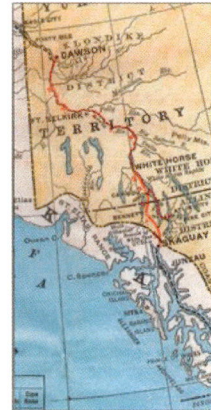

For Today

Just for today,
I will not ask God for anything until
I've thanked Him for everything He's already given.

Lonesome Dove

Lonesome Dove strutted, pecked, and bobbed through my backyard this morning. He's become a regular visitor but still spooks easily if we move too fast inside the house or make the tiniest noise. I like to watch him and usually stop my current chore to enjoy his visit.

Lonesome likes to begin his scavenger hunt at the Evans smorgasbord by poking around the base of the bird feeder for scattered tidbits. After he's munched on fallen sunflower seeds, he flaps clumsily to the edge of the birdbath for a quick drink of water and a stint of preening.

He looks ridiculous perched on a ledge meant for robins, but he doesn't seem to care, and I haven't had the heart to tell him.

If you haven't guessed, he's not really a dove, but he does seem to be lonesome. I think his mother forgot to tell him turkeys are supposed to travel in rafters, especially in the woods where mountain lions, coyotes, and hunters search for prey.

I've often wondered why Lonesome travels alone. Was he separated from his group by a youthful act of ignorance? Was he pushed out by a fully grown gobbler who wanted the hens for himself? And, why didn't he find a couple of jakes to hang out with while he waited for his own mating signal to begin? Maybe he doesn't know how to attract feathers of his kind.

He probably won't survive the spring if he can't find companions. One time the dog was loose and scared Lonesome into spreading his broad wings and thundering up to the lowest branch on the highest tree. Even knowing he can fly leaves me worried. Who will watch his back and warn him when predators slink in from behind?

Perhaps this solitary figure inspires lingering thoughts because my Christian walk frequently leaves me feeling alone and looking like something I'm not. After years of creating community ministries and then financing and fulfilling them by myself, I've often felt like the human version of Lonesome Dove.

How many times has my heart ached for a nice church ministry with carpeting, curriculum, camaraderie, and free advertising? How many times have I asked God why He sends a shy, insecure person on such an isolated path? The gifts of leadership are at work in my life, but when I turn to the right or left or look behind me, no one's following or working alongside.

I've also wondered if anyone is watching this sojourner from a hidden distance and if they're mocking my solo forays into unmarked ministry. I'm sure God knows but chooses not to tell me how many spy in silence, how many scoff, or how many have called on His name because they've seen His grace at work in my life.

Lord, I feel no presence beside my own, yet I KNOW you never leave me nor forsake me. If the enemy should come to pluck my life before its time, you will lift me to the Rock that is higher than I. Give me the courage I need to walk the path you've laid out before me. Amen and amen.

Dream's Journey

Birthed in her soul, I thought I'd be strong
but the Spirit whispered my end all along.
The call came and the journey began
through trials and tests by God's holy plan.

The desert stretched first before my path,
it seared and burned like the fueled wrath
of a God whose will would have to show
and let my glimpse of glory begin to re-grow.

The fiery trial ended at mountains steep.
Brokenness stood still to look up and weep,
"How could I soar in such a humbled state?"
Perhaps the journey will have to wait
until a day of strength and more power
a timely pick of human hour.

Grace came and lent a hand
God's call was strong—His time would stand.

Shattered and broken at last I arrived
at mountain's top so barren and deprived.
No commandments waited, no transfiguration,
just a stone altar with dread imagination.

"There's the thicket, but where is the ram?
Where's the rescue from the great I AM?"
Lying down pressed cold against the rock
to which I'd surely been sent
the dagger raised and found its mark:
the flickering flame of dream's broken heart.

Not my life, but His in me
flaming on 'til true liberty
unmasks God's best, His glory, His life,
revealed beneath the Master's knife.

Let Me Be a Wildflower

Every spring, California lupine covers the hill next to my home. The purple wildflowers are an awesome sight; they put a smile on my face and a bounce in my step.

A "volunteer" is someone who offers to do something without receiving any compensation for the work provided. Grandma used to call plants that popped up in unusual places "volunteers" because they choose to grow where no one planted them.

Lord, let me be a wildflower in someone's life today. May my unexpected appearance brighten the countenance of someone's heart and lend them strength for their journey. Amen.

Surprised by Life

How well I remember when my baby girl's life began. My son was an energetic nine month-old and my marriage was in its first crisis. That's when the unexpected loss of strength and morning sickness clearly signaled the presence of someone new. The phone rang at 8:32 on a Wednesday morning with news I didn't want to hear.[8]

"I'm calling to confirm you're pregnant." The nurse hesitated, perhaps remembering my tears when I arrived for the test, then continued softly, "Do you want to continue this pregnancy?"

"Of course!" I mouthed the right words while my heart fluttered in fear. This was not a good time for another baby.

Living out those words meant spending the better part of the next seven months in bed. While God knit together a baby girl in my unwilling womb, she prepared for life by siphoning off every ounce of my get-up-and-go.

The delivery ended the first difficult phase of a new life but immediately began another. My bundle of joy came out screaming, had her days and nights mixed up, and suffered from a serious case of colic. Everyone promised it would pass by the time she was three months old. Although it could have, it didn't.

Colicky kids can't explain what hurts or offer suggestions as to what might help, so I tried everything I read as well as everyone's seasoned advice: chamomile tea, long rides in the car, the constant hum of a vacuum cleaner. I kept Missy full, clean, moving, entertained, busy. I did everything and anything I could think of to alleviate her misery.

Eventually, I learned to function quite well with her glued to my hip since that seemed to be her favorite place to dwell.

The invisible umbilical cord snapped when kindergarten teachers insisted she leave my arms and walk into the classroom. Without a backward glance, she did. How quiet the house sounded. How strange to stand straight or cook a meal with two free hands.

School was hard for her. She was tested for dyslexia, hearing problems, and attention deficit disorder. None explained her inability to follow directions or complete assignments. My husband patiently tried to help with her homework; I couldn't get her creative spirit to sit still long enough to learn.

Then, just in the nick of time, Missy was assigned to a third-grade teacher who made a lasting difference. This steel-spined teacher decided that since there were no physical reasons for her not to do the work, she would. She could and she did. She made the honor roll for the first time in her four-year school career. We were proud. Grateful. Relieved.

Because of me, life continued to be hard for my strong-willed tomboy. I dressed her in ruffled dresses and set her long blonde hair in pink sponge curlers.

"Why?" she would whine, twirling her curls petulantly.

"Because I said so," was the stock answer.

Her knees, with their crisscross scars in various stages of healing, bore the brunt of my wish for a dainty, golden-haired princess. Like a mini-god, I continued to lay out the quiet, ladylike personality I wanted her to wear. Like a free-willed creation, she chose time after time to disregard its limits.

Then somewhere close to her thirteenth birthday, I realized I had stopped trying to create Melissa in my image. Somewhere along the way, I had begun to respect the strength of her character, her willingness to get in someone's face, and her winsome, independent spirit. In spite of all my convoluted efforts, she had found her identity, picked it up, put it on, and wore it well.

Even more amazing, somewhere in our shared journey, I found myself trying to emulate her kind of courage. And, in the trying, I found that she helped create a new image for me.

Melissa is a young woman now. She's bright and beautiful and always ready to GO somewhere or DO something. She's the one who moves when the phone rings or someone knocks at the door or there's a rap at the kitchen window. From experience, we suspect the visitor is there to see the only one living in our house who never says "no" to action.

Last month I had surgery. I was in a lot of pain and didn't want visitors. She disobeyed and came anyway. While my husband talked with the doctor in the hallway, she rested her chin on the handrails and silently watched me struggle for air. With tears filling her blue, blue eyes, she shyly pulled her childhood blankie out of a gaudy, oversized purse. After carefully tucking it around my shoulders, she kissed me on the cheek and left.

The blanket was soft and smelled like her. I was glad she disobeyed. Glad she came.

Do I want to continue this pregnancy? The words echo in my head from long ago.

What would life have been like without her? I wouldn't know that a woman can laugh with her teeth showing and still be considered a lady. Wouldn't have a shopping partner who doesn't drop and never stops. Wouldn't have a friend who's willing to see *Phantom of the Opera* five times. Wouldn't know that I've given the world a great gift. Or, that the gift I had a chance to give was given to me first.

Yes, today, and every day, I continue to be surprised by the advent and epiphany of life.

The Lord is My Shepherd

Psalm 23 [King James Version]

The Lord is my shepherd; I shall not want.

He maketh me to lie down in green pastures;
he leadeth me beside the still waters.

He restoreth my soul;
he leadeth me in the paths of righteousness for his name's sake.

Yea, though I walk through the valley of the shadow of death,
I will fear no evil; for thou art with me;
thy rod and thy staff they comfort me.

Thou preparest a table before me in the presence of mine enemies;
thou anointest my head with oil;
my cup runneth over.

Surely goodness and mercy shall follow me all the days of my life;
and I will dwell in the house of the Lord forever.

Saved

From 2 Samuel 22 (MSG)

"But me he caught—reached all the way from sky to sea; he pulled me out. (17)

"He stood me up on a wide-open field; I stood there saved— surprised to be loved! (20)

"God made my life complete when I placed all the pieces before him. ... he gave me a fresh start. (21)

"I feel put back together, and I'm watching my step. God rewrote the text of my life when I opened the book of my heart to his eyes." (23–24)

Lost and Found

Morning offered no hints that this day would be different than any other Wednesday—that it would be overwhelmed by every parent's worst nightmare or teach me lessons I'd never forget.[9]

Just as I slid the last dumpling into the simmering chicken soup, five-year-old Melissa burst into the kitchen.

"Mommy, I'm gonna get the newspaper, 'kay?"

"Matt, can you go with her?"

"I've got Royal Rangers tonight and gotta get this math done." My seven-year-old son sat at the kitchen counter surrounded by homework.

I pointed a finger still caked in sticky dough and warned her, "Okay, but come right back! No lollygagging!"

Her blonde pigtails bobbed in agreement. I almost smiled and made a mental note to redo her hair before church as she banged the door into the outside wall on her way out. This was the first time my baby would carry out this evening chore alone.

And because it never occurred to me that Robert Dunton, a recently released felon, would be passing our driveway in his station wagon, would spot Melissa, chase her, catch her, toss her in his car, and drive away—I didn't worry.

We knew something was wrong right away: the walk took ten minutes and she wasn't back in fifteen. My husband hiked down and saw the mail untouched in its box and the newspaper lying on the gravel.

While he was gone, I checked her bedroom, closets, and other common hiding places in case she'd slipped into the house unnoticed.

Soon all three of us, as well as our few-and-far-between neighbors, were searching for her.

The sun seemed to sink faster than usual that day, and the chilly fall air further dampened our sagging spirits. Against the backdrop of nature's twilight sounds, hollow voices continuously threw her name against the darkness. No answer bounced back.

Hours later, we met in the garage. No one dared to say it, but we had all lost hope.

"Let's pray," my husband whispered as he reached for our hands.

Mike's prayer was simple. "God, help us find Melissa. Your eyes can see her, ours can't. Keep her safe and show us where to look."

With that, we turned back toward the open garage door. Where do you look when you've already looked everywhere two, three, or four times?

As we stood paralyzed with fear and indecision, the phone rang. Mike grabbed the outside handset and I listened to his side of the conversation.

"Who is this?"

"Describe her to me."

"I don't understand who this is."

She's been kidnapped and this is our ransom call, I thought. *What kind of price tag will they put on our daughter's head?* In that same instant, I knew whatever they asked for, I would pay it.

The call wasn't the kidnapper but the California Highway Patrol. They'd found a little girl miles from our home and wanted to know if our daughter was missing. The dispatcher didn't have many facts but wanted us to meet the officer and the towheaded tyke where she'd been found.

Before we pulled off the freeway, we could see numerous police cars parked along the frontage road. They were parked at all angles and some still had their red-white-and-blue lights spinning.

I willed myself out of the car wondering how Melissa could possibly have gotten so far from home. Mike looked for the person in charge while I scanned the scene for her.

I spotted her in the backseat of a police car about the same time she saw me.

"Mommy, Mommy," she mouthed while pounding on the locked door.

A sheriff let her out and she jumped into my arms. I held her trembling body while she told me how Dunton grabbed her and how she'd fought against his grasp.

"I just got out of prison for killing my wife and baby," he told her. "If you don't shut up, I'll kill you too."

"I'm never gonna see my mommy and daddy again," she sobbed back.

It appears Dunton became disoriented after snatching Melissa and zagged around on curving country roads for a while. Eventually, his turns landed him on a boulevard that would take him to the freeway. Just as he turned toward a clean getaway, God gave us our miracle.

A California Highway Patrolman pulled out behind Dunton's vehicle and noticed the battered car was missing a taillight. Officer Thompson admitted since it was time to clock out, he decided to let the minor infraction slide. He later wrote in his report when he passed the station wagon, it "veered suspiciously onto the shoulder of the road." The evasive action as well as the driver's averted glance troubled him, so he decided to investigate using the taillight as an excuse.

Inside the stopped vehicle, he found an unkempt young man and a child he hadn't seen while passing.

"He took me from my mommy and daddy," the little girl kept crying.

Dunton tried to excuse her tears, but the officer didn't believe him. Officer Thompson cuffed him and gently tried to find out who the youngster was and where she belonged.

Four hours after the ordeal began, we all knelt by Melissa's bed and thanked God for the grace He chose to send. Public servants, family, and friends agreed: we would have never seen her again if God hadn't intervened.

Months later—after court appearances and sentencing, after we had returned to our normal work and school routines—I still struggled. Why had God allowed this?

One fogless morning, He answered.

He took me back to the "ransom" call and my oath to buy her back no matter what the cost. Then, He spoke to me in the quiet place only He is heard.

"Would you really have paid any price to get her back?"

"Absolutely."

"Would you have sold your home? Sold everything you have and emptied your bank accounts?"

"Yes."

"Would you have borrowed money and gone into debt?" He probed.

"Yes, I'd have worked for the rest of my life to pay back loans."

Heaven paused for just a moment before the final question, *"Would you have given your son?"*

My heart recoiled. How could I choose one child over another, and why would God ask me to do such a thing?

Slowly, the truth of His heavenly analogy broke open.

For just moments, I could feel the depth of God's sacrifice and grief as He sent Jesus to a manger and Calvary's cross. Jesus didn't just come, God gave. He gave one perfect child to release those taken and lost to His embrace. "For God so loved the world that he gave his only Son, that whoever believes in him should not perish but have eternal life" (John 3:16).

Mike and I have been married since 1971 and currently live in Pine Grove, California.
Our son, Matt, teaches chemistry at a California college;
our daughter, Melissa, is the editor for a Southern California newspaper.
God is good and we are grateful!

Before you close the book and put it away, may I pray with you?

If you're going through a season of darkness right now:

> **Lord**, let the one who holds this book feel your presence. Let her KNOW you see, you hear, you understand, and you have plans to deliver. In the name of Jesus, I ask for wholeness, healing, and restoration. Wrap your wonderful grace around her hurting heart and plant seeds of anticipation within. May she discover the peace that far surpasses human understanding. May she praise you in spite of her circumstances and begin to bloom where she is planted. May she KNOW your plan will prevail; a plan with purpose and blessings. In the name of Jesus, we ask with confidence. Amen.

If this book has inspired you to give your life to God in a new way, I suggest you pray this prayer out loud and write the date in the margin! Then, call someone and tell them you just prayed the Sinner's Prayer and want to confess with your lips that Jesus is Lord:

> **Father in heaven**, thank you for giving your Son so I could be restored to my place in your family. Jesus, thank you for dying on the cross in my place and paying the price of my redemption. Please forgive my sins and give me the gift of eternal life. I give you my life and ask that you spend it to bring glory to your name. Holy Spirit, come into my heart, be my guarantee of a heavenly destiny. Convict me, lead me, comfort me, and teach me God's ways. In the name of Jesus, amen.

Endnotes

[1] Blooming in the Dark, page 19; first published:
Bonnie Evans, "Glory in the Morning," *Evangel* 115, no. 21, 5–6.

[2] Leeches and Fungi, page 30; first published:
Bonnie Evans, "Relationship Metaphors from Nature," *Psychology for Living* 51, no. 3, 6–8.

[3] Jacob's Hug, page 36; first published:
This first appeared as a featured column on the editorial page of *The Gilroy Dispatch*, June 15, 2005.

The piece was revised and published:
Bonnie Evans, "What Lies Within," *Purpose* 43, no. 2, 6–7.

Reprint published in: *Standard*

Was reworked and included in *Soul Searchin'*

[4] The Bear Family, page 45:
The scrapbook disappeared when my parents moved and I consider it a deep loss. It would have given me great pleasure to include one of my father's poems with this booklet.

[5] Journey of Hope, page 46; first published:
Bonnie Evans, "I Stopped Doing and Started Being," *Decision Magazine* 40, no. 3, 10–11.

I considered it a great honor to be published in Billy Graham's magazine! Later versions of the article were reprinted in: *Evangel*, *Standard*, *The Vision*, and *Live*.

[6] The Twelfth Day, page 50; simultaneous publications in:

Bonnie Evans, "The Twelfth Day," *Purpose*, Vol. 42, No. 11, pages 4-5.

Bonnie Evans, "The Twelfth Day," *Standard*, Vol. 75, No. 47, page 5.

[7] The Best is Yet to Come, page 52; first published:
    This piece first appeared as a featured column in *The Gilroy Dispatch*, June 6, 2006.

    Was reworked and included in *Soul Searchin'*

[8] Surprised by Life, page 65; first published:
    Bonnie Evans, "Surprised by Life," *Celebrate Life* (March–October 2009): 10–12.

[9] Lost and Found, page 70:
    The events in this story took place on November 19, 1980. The testimony has been shared in youth groups, churches, and women's organizations.

    The first partial version of this story was published:
    Bonnie Evans, "In the Palm of His Hand," *Good News Broadcaster* 44, no. 2,54–55.

    The story was rewritten and the full version published:
    Bonnie Evans, "Lost and Found," *LIVE* 85, no. 1, pt. 4, 2–7.

    Reprints were published in: *Standard*, *Now What?*, and *War Cry*.

    A shortened version of it appears in *Soul Searchin'*

For more information about *Legacies* or to order books
published by Bonnie Evans

http://www.BonnieEvansLegacies.com

bonniere@gmail.com

Legacies
Preserving Memories of Ordinary People
Pine Grove. California

Titles by this author:

Blooming in the Dark – A book of encouragement for those going through hard times
(Available for Kindle, see website for link)

Soul Searchin' – A collection of conservative newspaper columns

Now I Lay Me Down to Sleep – a ministry tool for hospice patients and their caregivers

The Story Savers Workbook – how to interview and record your significant memories or
those of someone you love

Prisoners of Hope (pamphlet) – to assure and encourage